Semen Retention

A MAN'S GUIDE TO SELF-DISCIPLINE & SELF-CONTROL

By Aaron Fields

ISBN: 978-1-953962-06-5

CONTENTS

Something To Think About Before You Read

"Semen is the basis of your existence, so don't waste it foolishly."

----------Aaron Fields

Word from the Author

Without self-motivation, a man can't achieve anything. Having self-motivation is an important life skill to have. The reason self-motivation is important for every man to have is because each man is unique and has a purpose in life. With that being said, a man should never waste his time on foolish things that won't elevate him. When you seek spiritual things first and you learn how to monetize your gifts, you'll see a lot of your dreams become a reality.

There are several things that can hinder a man from unlocking his true potential. One of them is the overindulgence in sexual activities. Sexual urges can be both powerful and dangerous. It can be rather difficult to stop yourself from ejaculating because showing self-control is one of the most difficult things a man can do. However, if you're able to show self-control, you can achieve just about anything in this world.

There are many ways to improve self-control and sexual restraint. You can read books, practice meditation, yoga, or even pray, just to name a few. Another powerful thing you can do that would be more practical is to abstain from masturbation and pornography. You can also refrain from having sexual intercourse with every woman you see. If you're not aware of semen retention, I encourage you to do some research on it. You may find that practicing semen retention can maximize your potential and perhaps improve every aspect of your life. It's important for men to understand that your semen is valuable. If you don't take your semen seriously, you may end up with some serious health issues or you'll end up being careless with the woman by inseminating her.

As men, we must understand the repercussions for the things we do. When it comes to ejaculation, it's important to know how valuable your semen is. From a spiritual standpoint, consider your semen as life force energy. Your life force energy should never be taken for granted. Why? Well, because your energy can be cultivated into something great. That's why it's important to develop the ability to restrain yourself. With that being said, always remember that none of us are perfect and we're going to make mistakes. Whenever you experience a moment of weakness, don't dwell on it too much. Focus on improving yourself and getting stronger as you move forward.

Why Are You Curious?

Why are so many men curious about the concept of semen retention and masturbation? What's the reason behind most men spending most of their time masturbating and having sex? I think this happens because men don't know themselves well enough and lack motivation to pursue greater things in life. What exacerbates the situation is the men's lack of understanding about women. The broken relationship structure between men and women is largely due to men's failure to understand women.

The problem with men in this society is that many of them have an unhealthy obsession with women. It's important to learn how to approach women appropriately with the understanding of who they are and how they operate. Knowing the nature of women can prevent you from getting into dangerous situations that could affect your future. Because of a lack of understanding about women, many men are losing their minds and ruining their lives.

As it pertains to semen retention, make sure you are thinking with your head and not your penis. As men, sometimes our sexual urges will take over if we're not careful. I get it, a woman's face, vagina, breast, lips and buttocks are some of the most beautiful traits a woman has physically. However, it's imperative that you put things in its proper perspective by being disciplined and showing self-control.

SHE'S A DESSERT, NOT THE MAIN COURSE

What exactly do I mean when I say a woman is a dessert, but not the main course? When dining out, your full course meal comprises multiple dishes. The first course is the appetizer and the main course is the primary food. Your main dish is where you get your nourishment and satisfaction. Remember, the main dish is why you came to the restaurant. Finally, you have the dessert. The dessert can be quite tasty and mouthwatering. However, the dessert is simply empty calories, and it's not something you should eat every day.

Now, try to apply this analogy in your life and with the women you deal with. You'll realize that the main dish represents your priorities in life. Put your pursuit of knowledge, wisdom, and spiritual understanding above your pursuit of women and sex. The more you work on yourself personally, professionally and spiritually, the better of a man you'll become. It also wouldn't hurt to optimize your earning potential. Without money, you can't govern yourself accordingly. A man must accumulate money for himself first so he can live a more comfortable life. Money is not the most important thing in the world, but being financially stable brings a level of calmness to your life. Once you know how your money is coming in, you can focus on other things. However, if you don't know how your money is flowing in, it'll be harder to focus on the other important aspects of your life.

Once again, the main dish represents the most important aspect of your life, not the dessert. Although the dessert is delicious, you can't eat it every single day. In fact, if you have dessert everyday you'll eventually get sick. Sadly, a lot of men don't understand this concept because they wake up every morning wanting dessert. You cannot allow your penis to do all the thinking for you. Be wise and use your mind and instincts to make the right decision. I promise it will serve you well in the future. Idolizing women is one of the biggest mistakes men make that lead to their demise. Although women are beautiful and fun, chasing and obsessing over them isn't worth it. Chase knowledge, seek wisdom, and continue to develop a spiritual connection with God.

HOW TO PRACTICE SEMEN RETENTION

To build yourself up physically, mentally, and spiritually, some men make it a declaration to practice semen retention. How long you decide to practice semen retention is totally going to be up to you. Now keep in mind there are different ways to practice semen retention. One way to practice semen retention is to not engage in pornography, or you can remain abstinence. Another way to practice semen retention is to engage in sexual activity or make love to the woman without ejaculating. Either way, your mental acuity, willpower and self-discipline will become a lot stronger the more you practice semen retention. The goal is for you to maintain as much sperm as possible.

Most men don't realize that constantly shooting out sperm drains a lot of your energy. Not to get too much into your reproductive health, but when you ejaculate, you shoot out a lot of nutrients (zinc, selenium, vitamin C, etc). If you're not careful, your immune system can suffer if you ejaculate excessively. Again, I won't go too deep into this because there is a ton of information out there

that goes more in depth, and I'd rather leave that to the

professionals.

GENDER WAR

Men, never insert yourself into a gender war with women because it's not healthy. The woman is not equal to the man, and the man is not equal to the woman. It's important to maintain self-control over yourself and the situation at all times. Sometimes, women are naturally inclined to argue back with you. That's why you should never to expect women to swallow their words. Their overly competitive spirit will manifest itself because they don't want to be seen as weak or appear to be wrong. It's essential for me to understand that arguing with a woman is pointless and it rarely leads to a solution. So why engage in an argument with a woman when you can simply walk away?

Have you ever said "no" to a woman who asked you out? If so, please be mindful and prepared for the criticism that may come your way, because she may not take rejection very well. If you're not interested in dating or having sex with the women that are interested in you, they might get angry. Don't be surprised if they accuse you of being a homosexual. Never be shocked if they accuse of hating your mother, hating your sister, or having a small penis. Their reaction to you rejecting them reveals that many of these women are more sexualized than some men. Now I must admit some of these women are not used to rejection. Why? Because most men are always saying yes to them as opposed to setting high standards and establishing boundaries. When you don't establish the rules of engagement as men, you become part of the problem. Gentlemen, as you learn how to discipline yourself sexually, watch how most of these women approach you. A woman will notice something unique about you when you're not thinking about sex.

Always remember that every successful man has never lost women by chasing money and his purpose. However, you will definitely lose in life chasing women. It's imperative for men to understand that there are not that many women out here worth pursuing. Now, are there exceptions to that rule? Yes, because there are plenty of women who are sweet, caring and respectful that are worth getting to know.

Have you ever rejected a woman before? If so, how well did she take it? Was it mature or immature? More importantly, how well did you handle it?

_____

_____

_____

_____

_____

_____

_____

_____

_____

_____

_____

_____

_____

5

THINK ABOUT WHAT'S MORE IMPORTANT

Gentlemen, when you ejaculate, not only it drains your energy, but it takes time to rebuild the sperm you just lost. For those of you that masturbate multiple times a day, refrain from doing that and start thinking about what's more important. Instead of constantly pleasuring yourself sexually all day, go out and be more productive with your life. Start a new hobby. Focus on your purpose. Develop a healthy mind and exercise. Work on monetizing your gifts. Always remember to understand the importance of your semen, especially when you're dealing with women.

Is there anything wrong with masturbation, per se? No, not necessarily. It's just a big problem when you become addicted to it. Masturbation shouldn't be on your mind constantly, so I suggest you think of better things to do with your time. Now, are you going to have a moment of weakness from time to time? Yes, but don't get in the habit of expelling your semen every day. Hell, if you're that horny, go out and meet a woman. Believe me, there are some decent women out here. You just have to look. Once you find her,

make sure you are safe, responsible, and having fun.

What Are Your Thoughts?

Do you think there is anything wrong with masturbation, per se? Please explain and express your thoughts.

_____

_____

_____

_____

_____

_____

_____

_____

_____

_____

_____

_____

_____

VALUE YOURSELF

Gentlemen, all you need to know about the concept of semen retention is the conquering of your sexual urges. You must overcome these urges by developing self-discipline. That way, when you finally decide to indulge in sexual activities with a woman, it'll have more effectiveness and more potency. Why do I say this? It's because as a man, you can't be conventional and kowtow to every woman you see. Just because a woman has a vagina doesn't mean you have to have sex with her, even if she wants you to. Guys listen, I love women and they are wonderful, but it makes no sense to hook up with every single woman you find attractive. Being overly infatuated with women is going to weaken you physically, mentally, and spiritually.

As I mentioned earlier, semen contains nutrients that the body needs, so if you're going to use up your semen, do it wisely. Hopefully, as you get older, smarter and more mature, you'll think less about your penis and more with your head. Therefore, you won't find yourself in many dangerous situations with women. The primary reason for most deceased or imprisoned men is not because of women; but the men's inability to resist women's influence and power. Understand that the woman is going to be one of the primary sources of temptation that society will use to destroy you. In order to combat this temptation, you must value your life by having self-discipline and maintaining self-control.

BE CAREFUL

As you keep growing and learning in life, you'll discover that many people think men are easily controlled by sex, money, and entertainment. Which makes sense because sex, money, and entertainment all correlate with one another. If you're a man that exhibits certain traits that the woman finds appealing to her, you become the primary target. Although it's great that women are attracted to you, still be mindful and keep a watchful eye because some women have a hidden agenda. Just because she tries to manipulate you into having sex with her doesn't mean you should fall for it. Once the woman sees that she can't control you with sex, it becomes a cultural shock to her and she won't know what to do with you. Therefore, the woman actually has to work hard to get to know you as a person. Is sex a beautiful thing? Yes, sex can be great, but it can also control you if you're not careful.

During your lifetime, when you meet women, some of them will approach you in a very kind and appealing way. Initially, they will try to get on your good side by seducing you. Then eventually, you'll make the mistake of making her your wife or, even worse, getting her pregnant because you thought she was "the one". It's imperative that you men understand this, especially the young men.

Don't put yourself in a position that will negatively affect your life forever. Love the woman, cherish the woman, and respect the woman, but please understand the nature of the woman. Most of these women are impulsive, fickle, and unpredictable. If the woman is not corrected, she will create chaos and confusion in your life.

Assume that the woman will not be held accountable for her actions. Therefore, it's important for the man to regulate and discipline himself even more. He must always take ownership and responsibility because depending on the woman to hold herself accountable is too risky.

DON'T LET SOCIETY SHAME YOU

Why are women praised and embraced when they choose to be abstinent, but when men do it, something is wrong with them? To answer that question, it's just the society we live in, unfortunately. Expect to be castigated for making responsible and authoritative decisions that don't adhere to the idolization of the woman.

It's interesting how individuals can belittle others because they got rejected. What it reveals is that so many people who claim to "respect" other people's decisions don't care to know what it actually means. When you reject a woman, she may reveal that her interest was in controlling you rather than getting to know you.

Not only you shouldn't let society shame you, never doubt yourself either. Don't let your singleness make you think raising your standards was a bad idea. As a man, you always want to be the best version of yourself. If the woman can't manipulate you, she may label you for not conforming to her feminine ideologies. Don't believe what the women in your life say if they don't care about you.

Remember, a woman is supposed to compliment your life, not bring

evil into it.

IT'S OKAY TO HAVE STANDARDS

What all men need to understand is that your life is a direct reflection of the standards you have for yourself and for the women you bring into your life. If a woman has red flags that could be harmful to you, it's best to end the relationship before it gets worse. Especially if she has no intentions of improving herself. The issue with men is that we have the tendency to look the other way when we see red flags, even though our intuition is already telling us to raise our standards. I'm not saying you should have incredibly high standards that are unrealistic, but you should at least have substantial standards.

If making God, your aspirations, and your health a priority over the woman disappoints her, do it with a smile on your face. As a result, you'll finally stop disappointing yourself because you've reclaimed your life back. If you are tired of being frustrated and confused with some of these women out here, one of the first things you need to do is work on yourself and embrace solitude.

There comes a point and time in a man's life when he has to address his own demons and toxicity. Sometimes in life, a man will have to be his own healer and his own champion. Why do I say this? Well, as a man, you can't always look for the world to pay you back, you can't always look for somebody to blame. You can't walk around with a victim mentality because society will not feel sorry for you. At some point, you must learn how to rescue yourself.

RESULTS OF SETTING HIGH STANDARDS

If a man raises his personal standards and sticks to it, his relational standards will rise. When a man sets high standards for himself, his life will become much easier and calmer. When a man sets high standards for himself, he will already know what his non-negotiables are. Suppose you're uninterested in women who regularly use drugs and alcohol. One day, you catch a glimpse of a woman you liked, drunk and smoking a joint. Although you probably didn't want to see that kind of behavior from her, at least you know now that she's not your type and you can move on to something else. Always remember that it's okay to reject a woman that doesn't fit your standards.

When a man expects more from himself, he won't have to always voice his standards and expectations to the women he's dealing with. Why? Because they will already know what's expected of them. Either the woman will respect it and give support, or she won't. Understand that you shouldn't be going back and forth with the woman trying to change her, especially if she doesn't want to. Rather than adding more chaos and confusion to your life, just remove yourself from her and end the relationship.

High standards start from within, not from other people. The reason most men are struggling with women today is because you guys put up with a lot of foolishness and stupidity from low-quality women. Yet, you guys wonder why you always end up miserable and heartbroken. Once you know your non-negotiables, you won't have to express your standards because others will already know.

Although having sex with women can be a beautiful thing, a man should not make it the center of his life. Don't let your semen control you, you control the semen. Practicing semen retention will allow you to work on the underlying issues of codependency. Practicing semen retention will help you regain your autonomy and self-esteem. By practicing semen retention, you'll be able to manage your emotions, thinking, and sexual urges. When you spend more time ejaculating into a woman, or watching pornography, you'll place a lower priority on the important things you need in life.

As a man that's aspiring to improve, you should want more freedom, less drama, and self-respect. To gain self-respect, you must stay committed to your beliefs, keep your promises, and don't conform to the ideologies society throws at you.

For this activity, write down everything that you wish to achieve in this world. Then, write down everything that is preventing you from making this come to fruition. Think about what you could be and become.

_____

_____

_____

_____

_____

_____

_____

_____

_____

_____

_____

_____

_____

_____

_____

_____

_____

_____

SEMEN RETENTION IN A RELATIONSHIP

If you're in a relationship with a woman, you can't just suddenly cut off the sex from her. Why? It's like cutting off food, water and shelter from her because sex is a necessity in a relationship. If you're going to practice semen retention, do it when you're single. For those that are spiritual and adhere to the scriptures, you'll find that in **1 Corinthians 7:4-5**, it states that neither the man nor the woman have power and authority over their own body and to not deprive each other except by mutual consent. This means that your significant other does have power over your body, just like you have power over hers. What does this mean for you? It means that when your significant other wants sex from you, it's your job as a man to provide that for her because that's part of the relationship (mutual submission). If there's a situation where having sex isn't the best decision, that's perfectly okay. You don't want to force it.

It's important to understand that a relationship is not supposed to be about doing whatever you want all the time. Understand that there's nothing wrong with pleasing your woman, especially if she's not being toxic to you in the relationship. Now, even though women can be toxic, a lot of men out here are toxic too. Men, if you are a toxic person, leave women alone. Embrace solitude, practice semen retention and do whatever it is you need to do to get your life in order before you start a serious relationship with someone.

For this activity, list five things that you will no longer accept and tolerate. Don't forget to explain why.

1.

2.

3.

4.

5.

_____

_____

_____

_____

_____

_____

_____

_____

EMPOWER YOURSELF

As I mentioned earlier, the woman is the dessert, not the main course of the meal. You are at the best part of your life as a man when you are no longer controlled by this world through sexual gratification. Part of being a man is not allowing women to distract you from your purpose and your goals in life. That's why I mentioned earlier that most women are way more sexual than some of these men out here. Society will purposely condemn men by claiming that they are all over sexualized. Although that statement holds some validity, we can't forget that many women are also excessively obsessed with sex. How often do you see men walking down the street everyday showing their genitals for the public to see? In most cases, it's usually the woman showing off her vagina, breasts, stomach, and booty for other people to see. Why is that? Well, that's how some women attempt to fling their attraction.

The reason most women crave attention in various ways is because they are conditioned to captivate men through sex and by their physical appearance. Keep in mind this is what most women do. Therefore, if you're a man of wisdom and integrity, you'll realize that some of these women have little to offer you other than sex. Most men that have wisdom understand that a woman is more than just her sexual appearance.

Now, if you're dealing with a woman that you're not serious about, don't make the mistake of planting your seed into her. I say this because it's important for you guys to understand the situations you're in before they happen. You don't want to end up having unplanned children with a woman you've never held in high regard. The world doesn't need more children being raised in unhealthy environments with two parents that don't seem to respect each other. These are the situations that can be avoided when the man empowers himself by thinking and conducting himself on a much higher level.

FINAL MESSAGE

Yes, the purpose of semen retention is to keep your seed and not ejaculate excessively. Another aspect of semen retention that needs to be discussed more is the art of discretion and carefulness. In other words, be selective and strategic on the women you choose to sleep with. Once again, just because she has a vagina doesn't mean you have to have sex with her. There are women who are wife material, and there are other women who are not. When a man is selective about how he spreads his seed and he does it with caution, many people will be shocked and confused. Just because you're a man doesn't mean you should automatically be honored and compelled to have sex with a random woman that is sexually attracted to you.

Once again, when you think with your head and not your penis, many of the problems you have will go away. Most of the mistakes you guys make are based on sexual interactions with these random women. Gentlemen, please understand that most of these women out here are looking to create chaos and confusion. Are there women out here that are loving, supportive and respectful? Yes, there are. However, it's important to understand that the average woman is replaceable. I encourage you men to get more spiritual and seek God first. When you do that, it'll be much easier for you to put certain things in its proper perspective.

A lot of you guys are going to have a hard time getting a woman. Instead of pursuing women first, I encourage you to pursue spiritual things or your relationship with God. At the very least, try to become healthy and stable in every aspect of your life before seeking a relationship with a woman. That way, when you have your life together, it'll be easier to develop a fruitful relationship with a woman. Gentlemen, be vigilant about the things you're exposed *to*. Ejaculation is a common occurrence in most men. Always remember that imperfection is a shared experience. As men, we already know what we need to improve *on*, it's just a matter of doing it.

Notes